INSIDE

Little Brother
BOOKS

Published 2019.
Little Brother Books, Ground Floor, 23 Southernhay East,
Exeter, Devon, EX1 1QL
Printed in Poland.
books@littlebrotherbooks.co.uk | www.littlebrotherbooks.co.uk

The Little Brother Books trademarks, logos, email and website
addresses and the GamesWarrior logo and imprint are sole and
exclusive properties of Little Brother Books Limited.

This is an unofficial and independently written book, the inclusion
of any logos, images, quotes and references does not imply
endorsement. Whilst every care has been taken in researching and

LEVEL 1
0 / 100

FREE PASS
TIER 1   ☆ 0 / 10

GESTED CHALLENGES

all Sky Platforms
0 / 7

opponent within 10s after using a Shad
0 / 200

of 2 - Ride the Slip Stream around Neo
0 / 1

BFK101
Not Ready

2

TEAM RUMBLE
☆ SQUADS
FILL

PLAY

FORTNITE, WHAT'S THAT?

Never played Fortnite before? Wondering what it is? Then read this now!

Are you new to the mad world of Fortnite? Do you even know what millions upon millions of daily players are doing on this thing they call The Island? No? Then pull up a seat and let us tell you about a little game called Fortnite Battle Royale.

The game itself was conceived as an off-shoot of another title called Fortnite Save The World, a co-operative based title that pitted four players against an army of creepy critters in a weird and wacky world where half the population has disappeared and the rest are battling thunderous storms by building something called Storm Shields in a bid to return Earth to its original state.

Released in September 2017, Fortnite Battle Royale was a standalone entity that was conceived as a direct response to the growing popularity of the Battle Royale genre, in particular a title by the name of PlayerUnknown's Battlegrounds, which pitted 100 players against each other in a gritty battle to the death. PUBG itself was actually featured in films such as The Hunger Games, and the dark Japanese film, Battle Royale.

When Epic Games saw just how popular PUBG was they acted fast to develop their own take on it – Fortnite Battle Royale. Whereas PUBG is quite dark and serious, and

FORTNITE

Patching...

definitely not suitable for anyone under the age of 18, Fortnite Battle Royale has a far more goofier, madcap sense of humour that's apparent in just about every facet of the game. Tomato Heads and Durr Burgers, anyone?

It's fun, and most importantly it's free. Well, kind of, because here's the catch. While the base game can be downloaded for absolutely nothing, Players are required to spend real world money if they want to gain access to certain items. Purchasing the Battle Pass, which will cost you 950 V-Bucks, grants this access. V-Bucks are the in-game currency, and 1,000 of them will set you back £7.99.

And it doesn't stop at the Battle Pass. Players can buy everything from additional costumes for their character, to new Harvesting Tools, Back Bling and Gliders, all of which will be explore in detail here in these pages. Now – and it really is important for us to stress this – you don't need to buy any of these things to enjoy the game, or get good at playing the game. They are purely cosmetic; don't ever feel you have to buy a new Character Skin just because someone says so!

Now sit back, and dig into the ultimate guide to the world's most popular game! ●

LET'S PLAY!

Fortnite: Battle Royale has taken over the world. It's available on pretty much every single gaming platform you can think of, which means you have so many different ways to experience the game, whether it's at home or on the go. Let's take a look at all of the devices Fortnite Battle Royale can be mastered on!

PLAYSTATION 4

Fortnite on PlayStation 4 comes in two different flavours – you can either go for the completely free version, Fortnite Battle Royale, or pay for the full experience, which includes the PvE mode Save The World. There are two versions of the full game on the PlayStation Store at the time of going to press.

The Standard Founders Pack will set you back £32.99, whereas the Deluxe edition of the game will cost you £49.99. The PS4 version of Fortnite supports Cross-Platform Play with players on Xbox, PC, Mac and the mobile versions of the game. If you're a PlayStation Plus subscriber then you are in for a treat with this exclusive and stylish skin for Fortnite Battle Royale.

The PlayStation version also has the PlayStation Plus Celebration Pack, which includes the Blue Fusion Contrail, and the Coaxial Blue Glider. These are really easy to download too, just search for Fortnite in the PlayStation Store and voila!

Oh, and if you're playing PlayStation 4 Pro you are in for a super-cool treat. The game renders at a native 1080p, scene lighting gets a massive boost and the visual effects are bumped up to whole new levels of eye-watering awesomeness.

XBOX ONE

Just like the PlayStation 4 version, Fortnite Battle Royale is completely free on the Xbox Games Store, but if you want to play Save The World it's going to cost you. At the time of going to press the Standard Founders Pack costs £34.99. The Deluxe Founders Pack includes all this plus a whole lot more and costs £49.99.

The Xbox version of the game also includes exclusive goodies for the Save The World mode, including Xbox Live inspired characters: Commando Renegade (Soldier), Guardian Knox (Constructor), Jade Assassin Sarah (Ninja), and Trailblazer Jess (Outlander).

Players on Xbox One can Crossplay with players on PlayStation 4, PC, Mac, mobile and Nintendo Switch. To Crossplay with other players make sure you link your Epic Games account with your Xbox Live account and then add the friends you want to compete with via the Epic Friends menu on the main menu of the game.

If you're playing on Xbox One X, then, similar to PlayStation 4 Pro, the game gets a graphical boost. It runs at full 4K resolution and 60 Frames Per Second (FPS). We think it looks pretty darn amazing and we're sure you'll agree too, folks.

NINTENDO SWITCH

Fortnite on Nintendo Switch only includes the Battle Royale mode, which is still free-to-play and lets you spend real-world cash in the game store to purchase the Battle Pass and other items. It does not feature the Save The World mode, and at the time of going to press Epic Games has said that it has no plans to include it anytime soon.

Now, for quite some time you could play Fortnite online for free, but as of September 2018 Players are now required to have a Nintendo Switch Online account if they want to experience Fortnite Battle Royale. If you have played the game on PlayStation, Xbox or PC then you'll have noticed that the Nintendo Switch isn't quite as powerful as its competitors.

Resolution is a tad lower and pop-up is far more frequent when playing the Switch in docked mode, but it's still the same great Fortnite experience you know and love, so don't let that put you off. However, if you are going to play the game in docked mode in front of the telly we recommend using the Pro Controller.

Like other versions of the game Fortnite Battle Royale on Nintendo Switch is Cross-Platform, meaning you can face-off against other players on PlayStation 4 PC, Mac, Xbox One and mobile devices!

PC AND MAC

Playing Fortnite on a desktop tends to be much more expensive than playing it on a console. Now before you panic, this isn't because there are more fees involved, it's because desktop and gaming rigs can sometimes cost a chunky sum of cash.

However, it's possible to build or buy a decent gaming rig on a budget, but if you want a machine with all the bells and whistles then you had better be prepared to pay a hefty amount of cash for it. Fortnite on PC and Mac isn't available on the widely popular game store Steam, and must be downloaded directly from the official Epic Games' Store where you'll need to set up an Epic Games account that requires an active email address and password.

Once you've done that you're all set to start playing the game! If you're playing on a MAC it's also worth noting that Fortnite Battle Royale will probably not run on your machine if you're using Yosemite or El Capitan. Your Mac must also support Metal API, which can be checked on the official Apple website.

You can play the game with a keyboard and mouse, or you can hook up a controller, but be warned – PC Players tend to use a keyboard and mouse and they are good! Reaction times are just that bit faster using the preferred desktop method compared to a console's controller. Fortnite Battle Royale on desktop supports Cross-Platform play with Mac, Xbox One, PlayStation 4, Nintendo Switch and mobile devices, so that means you get to brawl on the island with EVERYONE!

MOBILE DEVICES

You want to game on the go? Then you should be grabbing Fortnite Battle Royale on Android, iOS and Tablet devices. Okay, it's not going to look as good as the consoles version, but who cares when you can still play it on a mobile device! Oh, and to make things that bit easier Epic Games has also added an Aim-Assist option, which helps when using your fingers to control your character AND trying to pick out enemies on the battlefield. It really is quite useful!

Other useful changes made during the transition from console to pocket and bag-sized devices include the nifty automated actions such as picking up items and opening doors. There are also footstep and gunshot indicators on the screen too, just in case you forgot your headphones on the bus to school and

want to play with your pals before class.

If you are running iOS then downloading and installing Fortnite Battle Royale is easy. You simply jump onto the App Store and grab it from there. If, however, you are using an Android device it's a slightly different story. You can't get the game on Google Play, you have to open an Internet browser on your device and go to www.fortnite.com/android where you will find directions to get the game up and running on your phone or tablet. It's super easy, and takes up 2GB of memory.

And once you have done that, you are all good to hit the Island and start chasing that Victory Royale. Oh, Fortnite Battle Royale on mobile devices does support Cross-Platform play with Mac, Xbox One, PlayStation 4, Nintendo Switch, PC and Mac Players.

THE BATTLE PASS

Understanding the Battle Pass in Fortnite Battle Royale.

Battle Passes are released at the start of every season in Fortnite Battle Royale. There are two tiers - Silver and Gold, with Silver being absolutely free (Yay!) and Gold requiring you to purchase the Battle Pass at the outset of each new season for 950 V-Bucks, which equates to about £7.99.

While some may frown at the cost of the Gold Tier Battle Pass, it's actually pretty reasonable given that it opens up the Gold Tier bonuses, which include awesome Character Skins, Experience Points Boosts, as well as rewards for levelling your character up.

Silver surfers

Sticking with the Silver Tier costs nothing and every player is granted access to it at the outset of the season in Fortnite Battle Royale. Rewards in Silver Tier are unlocked every four levels, and include items such as emotes and cosmetic harvesting tools,

so at least you are still earning goodies even if you don't want to want to spend any actual money on the game.

Level up

To level up your Battle Pass all you have to do is play matches and complete daily challenges to earn Experience Points, by taking out other Players on the battlefield and surviving matches. On top of Experience Points you can also grab Battle Stars, which are rewarded throughout a Season.

You get one Battle Star per level, but to encourage Players to keep coming back they get five bonus Battle Stars every five levels and ten Battle Stars every time you reach ten levels. The Battle is most certainly something you might want to consider. Or not. People play the game perfectly fine without forking out for one each month. ●

V-BUCKS

Getting to grips with Fortnite: Battle Royale's **in-game currency.**

It's important to remember that Fortnite Battle Royale won't cost you a penny to download, or play, but that doesn't mean there aren't ways to spend real-world money on the mountain of in-game goodies that Epic Games has made available since the game launched back in 2017. Just remember, all these Character Skins, Back Blings and Harvesting Tools won't do anything to enhance your abilities on the battlefield, folks. They are purely just for looking cool in a brawl!

SHOW ME THE MONEY

So, you want to buy some V-Bucks? Okay, let's take a look at what are they are worth in terms of real world money. Depending on your budget

V-Bucks come in multiple packages at the time of going to press. 1,000 will cost you £7.99, 2,500 costs £19.99, 6,000 equates to £49.99 and 10,000 will set you back a hefty £79.99. Yeah, it ain't cheap folks; so make sure you get permission from a parent or guardian before you go spending actual money on this in-game currency.

EARNING V-BUCKS

You can actually earn V-Bucks in the game, although it's usually very little. Some Battle Passes offer V-Buck rewards in the Gold Tier once you pass a certain level. Playing Fortnite Save The World (turn to Page 70 for more info on this if you've never heard of it!) is a great way to earn V-Bucks. All you have to do is grab the Daily Login Rewards, take on the Daily Quests, and beat Storm Shield Defence Missions.

And now you know all about the V-Bucks. Go forth and start earing 'em, soldier! ●

ARENA

Your guide to **getting to grips** with Fortnite Battle Royale's Arena Mode!

I ntroduced back in Season 8 with Update v8.20, Fortnite Battle Royale's Arena Mode is to some extent a ranked game mode that allows you compete with competitive Players from around the world. There are some pretty cool opportunities to be had, including the ability to nab a space in major global Fortnite tournaments, and land some cold hard cash that can be spent on whatever you want.

Heck, if you're good enough you might even be able to snag enough real world Loot to buy a kick-ass gaming rig. But, let's be honest here – it won't be easy. There are Players out there in the world that are crazy good at this game. They are called Professionals for a reason, so just remember that and don't let it get in the way of life, friends and, most importantly, your schoolwork!

ARENA MODE EXPLAINED

Arena Mode consists of either Solo or Duo Modes, and they are permanent. That means that they never disappear, unlike some of the other Limited Time Modes we discuss in

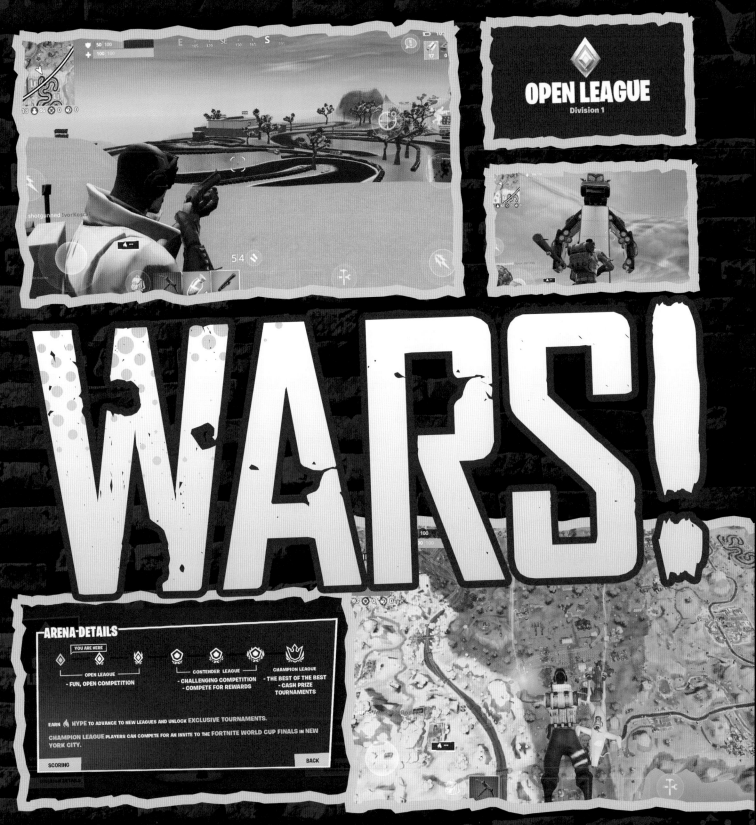

WARS!

ARENA-DETAILS

YOU ARE HERE

OPEN LEAGUE
- FUN, OPEN COMPETITION

CONTENDER LEAGUE
- CHALLENGING COMPETITION
- COMPETE FOR REWARDS

CHAMPION LEAGUE
- THE BEST OF THE BEST
- CASH PRIZE TOURNAMENTS

EARN 🔥 HYPE TO ADVANCE TO NEW LEAGUES AND UNLOCK EXCLUSIVE TOURNAMENTS.

CHAMPION LEAGUE PLAYERS CAN COMPETE FOR AN INVITE TO THE FORTNITE WORLD CUP FINALS IN NEW YORK CITY.

SCORING   BACK

these pages. In Arena Players are ranked by Division. Everyone begins Arena Mode in Division 1. Players can rank up to Division 7 from here.

In order to rank up, Players need to accumulate Hype, which is based on the number of Players they take down in a match, as well as where they finish on the Scoreboard by the game the match comes to an end. Earning a certain number of Hype points allows Players to jump up a rank, so, if you're playing, always remember to go after those Hype Points like it was your only mission in life!

THE DIVISION (S)

Arena Mode has 7 Divisions that fall under Open League, Contender League and Champion League. Divisions 1 to 3

are part of the Open League, Divisions 4 to 6 are part of the Contender League and Division 7 is where the best of the best come to play. If you make it into Division 7, you had better be prepared, because things can get pretty tough in here.

In terms of Hype Points required to move through the Divisions in Arena Mode, Player start with 0 Hype Points and eventually climb to a total of 300 plus, which can only be achieved once the Champion League has been cracked. Arena Mode is a fantastic addition to the world of Fortnite Battle Royale, and, with enough practice and dedication, could also open the door to the Fortnite Battle Royale World Cup. So if you do take part in it, we wish you the best of luck! ●

RARITY EXPLAINED

Understanding the **many different** Fortnite Battle Royale **weapon types!**

When you first power up Fortnite Battle Royale and see weapons sporting different coloured descriptions you might be wondering what in the hell is going on. Weapon Rarity is a common trope in the world of free to play games such as Fortnite... so don't panic, Player! We are here to explain the five different rarities that can be obtained from the likes of Loot Chests, downed enemies, Vending Machines and stuffed Supply Drops.

Common

Common weapons are, well, the most common kind you can find in the game. They're pretty much littered everywhere across the vast map, and are distinguishable by their Grey coloured description boxes. Weaponry that falls into the Common category includes the Tactical Shotgun, Assault Rifle and Pistol.

Backpack full!
Legendary | Consumable
BUSH

169   0   34

Uncommon

Uncommon weaponry spawns less than Common weaponry. It can be found in Loot Chests or spread around the map if you search your landing spot. They are distinguishable by the Green coloured description boxes. Uncommon weapons include Dynamite, Silenced Pistol, Pump shotgun, as well as Assault Rifles and Tactical Shotguns.

Rare

Now, this is where things start to get a little trickier Fortnite fans. Rare weapons are not as easy to find as Common or Uncommon. They can be grabbed from Loot Chests, Vending Machines, downed enemies and, sometimes, on the ground... if you are lucky enough. They're pretty easy to spot too, thanks to the bright Blue description box. Weapons in this category include Grenade Launchers and Dual Pistols.

Epic

Epic weapons are excellent for taking down other Players with Shields, because they pack quite the punch and can drain a Player's health with a few well-placed shots. You'll rarely find one of these on the ground, unless you took down an opponent and looted their dropped gear. They're mostly located in Loot Chests and Vending Machines, so be sure to search around to get your hands on 'em. Epic weapons include the Mini Gun, Assault Rifle and the mighty Hand Cannon.

Legendary

Legendary Rarity weapons are the most powerful of all on the battlefield. These bad boys can be found by taking out other Players and looting their gear, or in Loot Chests and Vending Machines. If you're facing down a Player wielding one of these, you might want to turn and hightail it out of there or it's game over, man! Legendary weapons include, Assault Rifles, Miniguns, Heavy Snipers and more. ●

BACKPACK, BACKPACK

Check out these cool Back Bling Backpacks from the Item Store!

CRYO HOPS

This Epic Rarity Back Bling features a frozen bunny rabbit inside a Cryo Chamber, and can be picked up by purchasing the Gemini character Skin in the Item Store. It will set you back a cool 1,500 V-Bucks. It also comes in two colours – blue and black. The Black Cryo Hops featured an angry bunny, if that's your jam?

BANANA BAG

Other Players on the battlefield will go, um, bananas for this super cool Back Bling. The Banana Bag came as part of the Marino Outfit, and features a bag with – you guessed it! – bananas in it, as well as a bottle of water. Shame we can't use the bananas as weapons in a match. That would be fun!

V6

Vroom, vroom! Get your hands on the roaring and awesome V6 Back Bling by snapping up the Mechanimal character Skin pack from the item store. It's basically a big 'ol engine, and it looks pretty cool if you ask us. It can be worn with other outfits too, and will set you back a chunk 1,500 V-Bucks.

DUAL KAMA

The Dual Kama Back Bling is pretty terrifying looking – it's basically two super huge blades attached to your character's back. Crazy, right? Released as part of The Falcon Clan Character Skin set this can be unlocked by purchasing the Kuno Skin set for 1,500 V-Bucks. These things really aren't cheap, are they?

OMISSION

Always look selectively discreet with this Back Bling, which was released as part of the Rare Psion Character Skin pack. It's also part of the Third Eye Set that includes the Psionic Edge Harvesting Tool, Disruptor Glider and an additional Back Bling called Commission. It will cost you 1,200 V-Bucks in the Item Store.

SNO CONE

The Sno Cone is the never-ending treat that just keeps on giving. This cutesy teddy bear holding a blue ice cream cone is part of the Lil Whip Character Skin that was released as part of the Two Scoops Set. Other ice cool items in the Set included the Ice Pop Harvesting Tool and Ice Cream Cruiser Glider.

HYPNOTIC

Other Players will have no option but to stare into the eyes of this bizarre Back Bling, giving you the opportunity to blast 'em when they're distracted by it! Released alongside the Mezmer Outfit and as part of the Sun Soldiers Set, this Back Bling can be paired with any Character Skin of your choice. For 1,200 V-Bucks.

TOME POUCH

Despite what you might think this pocket packed Back Bling doesn't allow for any extra storage. No Back Bling does. But it does look pretty darn cool strapped to your character's back. Released alongside the Elmira Character Skin Set, and as par of the Arcane Arts Set this one will costs you a chunky 1,500 V-Bucks.

SHRIMPY

Strap this tasty Sushi snack to your back on the Battlefield! To get this one you needed to pick up the Maki Master Character Skin that was released as part of the Sushi Masters Set. It also included the Filet Axe Harvesting Tool and the Flying Fish Glider. Next time you see this on the Item Store be prepared to pony up 1,200 V-Bucks!

EMBLAZONED

To the victor goes the spoils, the spoils of awesome Back Bling that is! Released as part of the Jaeger Character Skin that hit the Item Store with the Primal Hunters set, Emblazoned will cost you 1,500 V-Bucks. Other items in the set included the Battle Axe Harvesting Tool and the Tusk Glider. Prepare for battle!

WINGBACK

Oh how we do wish we could fly around the map with these awesome wings! Sadly, Back Bling is always a purely cosmetic item and has no impact whatsoever on the abilities of your character in a Fornite Battle Royale brawl. To own these you needed to snag the Mothman Character Skin that costs 1,500 V-Bucks.

FABLED CAPE

The Fabled Cape is kind of like Little Red Riding Hood's hooded cape. It's filled with patches and claw marks, presumably from the Big Bad Wolf trying to shred it! This pretty slick Back Bling was released during Season 6 of Fortnite Battle Royale, and to snag it you had to reach Tier 14 of the Free Battle Pass.

SPIDER SHIELD

Spun from endless strands of creepy spider webbing, this buggy looking Back Bling comes in the shape of a giant spider carapace, and also has big scary red eyes! Now, this may look like it's a shield, but be warned – this won't offer any protection on the battlefield. Plus it will cost you a very chunky 2,000 V-Bucks.

SCOPE SATCHEL

Oh man, the team at Epic Games sure do like to taunt us with cool things. Take the Scope Satchel for example. This rare Back Bling has so much coolness going on, including rifle bullets and sniper scope... that we can't even use in the game! Still, it does look great on a character while they're running around the map.

SHACKLED STONE

The Shackled Stone is pretty awesome in that when you pop it on your character for a match, it will change and emit a greenish spooky light once you have taken out a certain number of Players on the battlefield. Released as part of the Western Wilds Set, this Back Bling can be unlocked once you buy the Deadfire Skin.

CLOCKWORKS

Tick, tock, bang! You are out of the match! This very cool, and large, cuckoo clock Back Bling is pretty funny in that whenever you take an opponent on the battlefield out of the match it emits a sound. It's an Epic Rarity release, and will set you back 1,500 V-Bucks alongside the Ludwig Character Skin outfit. Cuckoo!

KICK DRUM

Get the whole band together with Kick Drum, the Epic Rarity Back Bling that comes with the Stage Slayer Character Skin, released as part of the Garage Band set alongside the Keytar Back Bling, Lead Swinger Harvesting Tool, and Hot Ride Glider. It'll cost you a trashin' 1,500 V-Bucks and it's super rock n' roll!

BOOMBOX

Pump up the volume on the battlefield with the Boombox Back Bling! This Epic Rarity piece of gear was released as part of the Spandex Squad Set, which also included the Windbreaker Glider and Axercise Harvesting Tool. To unlock this Back Bling you'll need to buy the Mullet Marauder Character Skin for 1,500 V-Bucks.

SUBJUGATOR

There's just something about this back bling that screams mean and scary, don't you think? Unlocked as part of the Enforcer Character Skin, to earn this one you will have had to have completed the Road Trip Challenges, which are pretty damn hard. Why? Because there are 49 in total! If you were one of the lucky ones who finished the Challenge and own this, we salute you.

ROAD READY

This Rare Back Bling getup can be unlocked once you pony up the 1,200 V-Bucks for the Backbone Character Skin, which was released as at part of the Biker Brigade Set. Sadly, and despite what it might look like, this Back Bling doesn't provide any sort of bonus storage for your character. It's all just for show, folks!

CLOBBERIN' TIME

Check out ten awesome **Harvesting Tools** in Fortnite Battle Royale!

1 Pot O Gold

The Pot O Gold is the perfect lucky charm on the battlefield. Use it for harvesting loot, or for whacking your enemy repeatedly until they've been knocked out of the match! Originally released for St. Patrick's Day, this one turned your harvesting tool into a magical enemy-bashing wand!

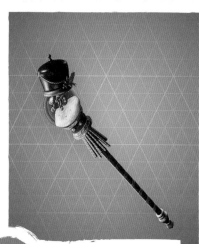

2 Snow Globe

Ho-ho-ho! Grab the Snow Globe and wish your enemies a very Merry Christmas before clocking them over the head with this fun and festive Harvesting Tool. The Snow Globe was released as part of the Nutcracker set during Christmas 2018 alongside some great skins and backpacks.

3 Rainbow Smash

Rainbow Smash is such a cool looking Harvesting Tool you can buy a full size replica of it! That said this is the part where we warn you not to use the replica to injure anyone in real life; save swinging that crazy unicorn head around for the battlefield, please!

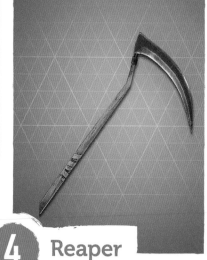

4 Reaper

You know how they say don't fear the reaper? Well scratch that, because if you see someone coming running towards you wielding this you had better run! Priced at 800 V-Bucks, this one was created alongside the cool John Wick inspired Reaper character skin.

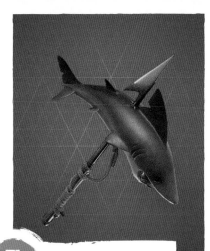

5 Chomp JR

Perfect for when you're playing Baby Shark on repeat while dishing it out to enemies on the battlefield, Chomp Jr turns your Harvesting Tool into a harpoon with a shark attached to the end of it. Um...okay. Anyway, it's fun to whack an enemy over the head with a shark!

6 Skull Sickle

The Skull Trooper character skin is one of the most popular in Fortnite, so it's no surprise that the accompanying Harvesting Tool has made our list. The Skull Sickle hit the Fortnite Store during Halloween 2018 alongside a host of cool items in the Skull Squad Set.

7 Six-String Striker

If you've got 1,200 V-Bucks kicking around then the Six String Striker is the Harvesting Tool for all you Mariachi fans out there. Released as part of the 2018 Mexican Day of the Dead set, this one is pretty damn cool if you ask us.

8 Lamp

Grab the Lamp and turn the lights out on an enemy by smacking 'em over the head with this rather lovely household object turned Fortnite Battle Royale weapon. If you've ever wanted to look good wielding some cool modern design, the Lamp is most definitely for you.

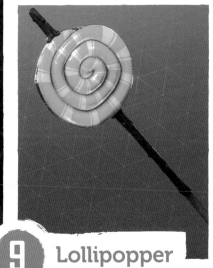

9 Lollipopper

For those of you on the battlefield with a penchant for sugary treats, the Lollipopper is the Harvesting Tool of your dreams. Released as part of the Sweet Tooth set the Lollipopper sported a dual colour lollipop that was green on one side and pink on the other.

10 Balloon Axe

Don't be misled by balloons. They might look weak, but this thing sure can do some damage once you start swinging it around the place. Released alongside the Party Parade set, this one got more than a few laughs when it arrived during Season 5.

ENTER THE ENDGAME

The Avengers and Fortnite combine forces to battle Thanos!

018 Fortnite and Marvel teamed up to bring
anos to the game in celebration of the release of
engers Infinity War. It was awesome, but the
gripe fans of both Avengers and Fortnite had
e Limited Time Mode was that only one player got
trol the Mad Titan.

if you were on the side trying to take him down to

get your hands on the Infinity Gauntlet he was massively
over-powered and possessed a seemingly limitless health
bar. If you did somehow manage to beat him and grab the
Gauntlet you then had every Player on the map chasing
after you to take you down and nab it for their own
nefarious purposes. In short, it really wasn't that much of a
Limited Time Mode to play.

Heroes & Villains

In the Endgame Limited Time Mode,
which arrived with Update 8.50 in
April earlier this year, the developers
changed things up quite a lot in order
to keep things interesting for everyone
on the battlefield. In this mode
Thanos and the Chitauri army have
invaded the island in search of the
Infinity Stones. One team plays as the
Heroes while the other team steps
into the role of the Chitauri army.

The Heroes have a helping hand in
the form of a treasure map that leads

rules are simple – the Heroes have to take down the Chitauri and Thanos, while the bad guys have to grab all the stones and wipe out the Heroes.

Crazy Crossover

The Fortnite and Avengers crossover event has definitely been one of the most thrilling and enjoyable Limited Time Modes to come to Epic's game in quite some time. It was significantly wilder than a standard Battle Royale match, but that was because of how insanely powerful

Thanos' attacks were, as well as the weaponry crafted for Earth's Mightiest Heroes. It's a shame this Limited Timed Mode has come to an end, because we'd love to play it all day, every day!

them to Mythic Avengers weapons wielded in the Marvel Cinematic Universe by Iron Man, Hawkeye, Thor and Captain America. The Chitauri on the other hand starts the brawl with a laser, anti-structure grenade and a jetpack.

Titan Smash!

The first Chitauri to find one of the Infinity Stones is transformed into Thanos, who packs a super punch, jump ability and a laser beam attack that can decimate anything in its sights. The more Infinity Stones Thanos finds the more powerful he becomes, while also powering up the Chitauri's health bar. From here, the

THANOS IS COMING! ELIMINATE HIS ARMY BEFORE HE GETS ALL SIX INFINITY STONES, OR HE WILL BE TOO STRONG TO FIGHT!

AVENGERS ASSEMBLE

A look at some of the Avengers **weaponry**, special **challenges** and comic book character **skins** that came with the Avenger's Endgame Limited Time Mode.

Stormbreaker

Stormbreaker is ripe for creating wanton destruction on the Battle Royale Island. Its primary attack is an axe swing, while its secondary attack is the ability to hurl it at the hordes of Chitauri and watch it shatter their evil alien skulls. It's also got a third capability that triggers while in the air – the mighty ground pound.

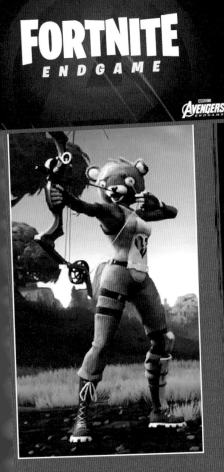

Hawkeye's Bow

Hawkeye's Bow is much trickier to master than the other weapons because of how precise you have to be in terms of aiming. The primary mode of fire is an explosive arrow, while the secondary one is a Grapple Arrow, which is basically a superhero spin on the regular Fortnite weapon, The Grappler.

Cap's Shield

Steve Rogers' iconic shield is the perfect weapon in the Limited Time Mode for offensive and defensive play on the battlefield. Holding down the fire button raises the shield so you can block incoming projectiles. Be warned, it doesn't offer 360-degree protection, so watch your back. Its secondary attack is Cap's signature shield throw, and it's awesome!

Repulsor Gauntlets

Iron Man's Repulsor Gauntlets come with a host of slick attributes, including the ability to hover like Tony Stark does, as well as blast enemies with lasers from the palms of the gauntlets. Another really cool feature is that enemies are targeted via the gauntlet's HUD reticule, which makes blasting bad guys much easier.

CONGRATULATIONS!

Thanks for playing Endgame! Enjoy!

GLIDER
AVENGERS QUINJET
Avengers assemble!

COLLECT AND CLOSE

CHALLENGES		
ENDGAME	0%	

6D 22H 47M

COMPLETION REWARDS

Complete **ANY 10 CHALLENGES** to earn the reward item. | 0 / 10

CHALLENGES

Deal damage while hovering with Iron Man's Repulsors	0 / 1,000	XP 500
Collect Infinity Stones	0 / 3	
Play matches of Endgame	1 / 7	
Deal damage by throwing Thor's Stormbreaker Axe	0 / 1,000	
Deal damage while flying with the Chitauri Jetpack	0 / 100	XP 500
Eliminations in different matches of Endgame	0 / 5	
Deal damage with Captain America's Shield	0 / 1,000	
Deal damage with the Chitauri Laser Rifle	0 / 500	XP 500

X

MARVEL | GLIDER
AVENGERS QUINJET
Avengers assemble!
Part of the **Avengers** set.

Quinjet Glider

One of the biggest pulls for fans of both Fortnite and Avengers was this – the Quinjet Glider, which could only be earned by completing ten specific Endgame challenges the development team cooked up for the release of the mega movie.

These included collecting Infinity Stones, blasting enemies with a Chitauri laser, slamming an enemy with Cap's shield or just playing a game of, er, Endgame.

MARVEL | OUTFIT
BLACK WIDOW OUTFIT
Whatever it takes.
Part of the **Avengers** set.
[Selectable Styles]

OWNED ✓   OWNED ✓

● 1,500
OWNED ✓

GET V-BUCKS

Black Widow

Alongside the fantastic mode Epic and Marvel collaborated on, the team released this rather awesome skin of the Black Widow, arguably one of Marvel's toughest superheroes despite actually having no superpowers. At the time of going to press it costs 1,500 V-Bucks. For an extra 800 V-bucks you got the Widow's Bite Harvesting Tool, while another 200 V-bucks snagged you her custom emote.

E IS FOR EMOTE

Counting down ten of the best Fortnite Battle Royale **Emotes** to date!

1

DANCE MOVES

It may be free, and it may be one of the most used Emotes in the game, but it sure is one of the most memorable – give it up for Dance Moves! Equip this one for your first match so you can jive to sounds of classic beats!

2

TAKE THE L

Take the L. Take it! This taunting Emote exploded onto the Fortnite scene during Season 3 when Players unlocked it after reaching Tier 31 of the Battle Pass. It's funny, it's goofy and we just love to use it whenever we take someone down.

3

FLOSS

Have you ever wanted to express yourself in a ludicrous way on the battlefield? Then you need the Floss Emote. This groovy move is seen a lot during a match, but it was only made available to Players via the Season 2 Battle Pass. Boo!

4

INFINITE DAB

The Infinite Dab is arguably one of the most iconic and popular Fortnite Emotes released to date. This Rare class Emote costs 500 V-Bucks in the Fortnite Shop and first appeared in July of 2018. Grab it next time you see it and dab all day long.

5 ORANGE JUSTICE

We're not sure what's orange or justice related about this one, but we love it! This ice cool Emote made its debut during Season 4 of Fortnite Battle Royale, and in order to earn it Players had to reach Level 26 by completing challenges.

6 ELECTRO SWING

Get your battlefield groove on with this classic old school swing dance move from yesteryear. This Rare Emote clocks in at 500 V-Bucks and first swung its way onto the Fortnite store back in October 2018. Keep an eye out for it if you dig it!

7 DANCE THERAPY

Feeling frustrated? Then just let it all out with the Dance Therapy Emote! This Epic rarity Emote first appeared in 2018 and, like a lot of the others on here, can be bought for 800 V-Bucks next time you see it surfacing on the Fortnite store.

8 ZANY

If you feel like getting a little weird in front of your enemies or teammates then the Zany Emote is the one for you! It lets you pull off a silly dance where your character raises their hands and leg. If this is your jam, it'll cost you 800 V-Bucks.

9 DISCO FEVER

Get ready to heat up the dance floor and the battlefield with Disco Fever, the disco-dancing taunt that's sure to rile your enemies after you take 'em down! Part of the Fortnite Fever set, this one will set you back a cool 800 V-Bucks.

10 PHONE IT IN

Lay down a saxy groove with this Emote that first appeared in version 6.31 of the game in December 2018. This Epic rarity Emote will set you back 800 V-Bucks and lets you pull a saxophone out of thin air before jamming wildly on it. Groovy!

SHOP 'TILL YOU DROP

We pull back the curtain on **goody-packed** the Games Store.

All Systems Operational

HELP

What can we help you with?

EPIC ACCOUNT · FORTNITE · EPIC GAMES STORE & LAUNCHER

OTHER EPIC PRODUCTS

Here's an interesting fact – Epic Games launched the Epic Games Store in January 2019, a digital shop accessed via your PC home computer to purchase games developed by the team at Epic, as well as games from other developers around the world. At the time of going to press, and in less than four months the store reported more than 85 million registered users.

You read that number right – 85 million in just four months. Let's try to put that in context: the PlayStation 4 has 90 million active monthly users that have been accumulated since the console was first released back in

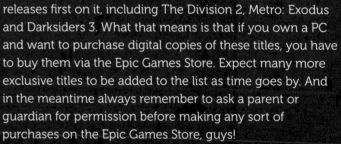

2013. It took Epic Games a mere quarter of a year to climb to the same dizzying heights. It's an incredible feat for the publisher, and it's likely this number will continue to grow.

Besides being a digital game shop, one of the great things about the Epic Games Store is how it works to benefit game developers, in particular smaller games companies that don't have huge budgets such as Ubisoft, Electronic Arts or Take Two. Epic Games takes only a 12% cut of the revenue, leaving 88% to the developer. This is huge compared to other digital game stores that tend to take up to 30% of the revenue from sales.

Okay, so that's very good news if you're a developer. What about members of the public? Don't worry, because every two weeks Epic Games hands out free games to registered users. To date there's been a whole bunch of excellent titles, including the deep sea diving simulator, Subnautica, the bonkers Super Meat Boy, the point and click adventure Thimbleweed Park and the excellent supernatural spook-fest Oxenfree. It's a pretty cool deal and it means users can build a slick collection of free games over time without spending a single penny.

Another feature of the Epic Games Store that sets it apart from the others is the huge swathe of exclusive content that releases first on it, including The Division 2, Metro: Exodus and Darksiders 3. What that means is that if you own a PC and want to purchase digital copies of these titles, you have to buy them via the Epic Games Store. Expect many more exclusive titles to be added to the list as time goes by. And in the meantime always remember to ask a parent or guardian for permission before making any sort of purchases on the Epic Games Store, guys!

Rocket League

Rocket League is quite possible the most fun you'll ever have playing football with cars! It's so crazy, so fast and so completely out there it shouldn't work. This is a multiplayer game at its finest, and one that should absolutely be played with your mates whenever possible. Get over to the Epic Games Store and grab it now!

EPIC GAMES

Check out some of the best games to **spend your hard-earned pocket money** on!

Shadow Complex

First released on the Xbox 360 in 2009, Shadow Complex was developed by Chair Entertainment and the team at Epic Games. It's a side-scrolling shoot 'em-up packed with plenty of action, boss battles and a great story with plenty of twists and turns. It's a must for anyone who might have missed it the first time around.

Journey

Originally released on PlayStation 3 all the way back in 2012, Journey was updated for PlayStation 4 consoles and now PC. This superb game casts you as a robed stranger wandering through the desert towards a mountain in the distance. It's beautiful, bold and absolutely brilliant; snap this up if you've yet to play it.

Oxenfree

Oxenfree is a supernatural mystery game developed by Night School Studio. There's so many ways the spooky narrative in this one can unfold it's ripe for replays, so if you do snag it don't put it to one side after that first play; with branching dialogues, and choices there's a lot to do and see.

Metro Exodus

Metro Exodus is arguably one of the most polished and beautiful looking games of the current generation. But if you're expecting a Call of Duty experience where you just blast your way through enemies this is not the game you're looking for. This one is a slow-burner guaranteed to have you on the edge of your seat!

World War Z

Argh, zombies – RUN! This is based on the smash hit movie from 2013, but to be quite honest it seems very odd that a game based on a movie comes out six years after the film's release date. The good news is it's a whole heap of fun, and kind of scary too. If you're not a fan of the walking dead then best avoid this one.

The Division 2

Ubisoft's apocalyptic shooter is ideal for playing with friends. It casts you as a super soldier in the aftermath of a viral outbreak. You have to work with your teammates to complete increasingly daring missions, grabbing stacks of loot and taking out hordes of bad guys roaming the streets of Washington D.C.

Borderlands 3

Borderlands 3 is the next chapter in the crazy colourful comic book inspired shooter from Gearbox Entertainment. This game is all about shooting stuff and grabbing loot; oh, and meeting wild and wacky characters along the way too. If you have a PC this one is available exclusively on the Epic Games Store too.

WINNER, WINNER

All the details on the first ever **Fortnite World Cup!**

WORLD CUP NEWS

APR 26, 2019

ONLINE OPEN WEEK 2 RECAP

APR 18, 2019

FORTNITE WORLD CUP - CREATIVE

APR 17, 2019

ONLINE OPEN WEEK 1 RECAP

SEE ALL

WORLD CUP

OVERVIEW · DETAILS · **SCHEDULE** · STANDINGS

SERVER REGION : EUROPE ▾

PENS, WEEK 1

ENS, WEEK 2

Okay, so you think you've got what it takes to be the best there is out there on The Island? Then the Fortnite World Cup is the tournament for you, competitor! First announced at the E3 Party Royale Pro-Am back in the summer of 2018, the Fortnite World Cup is open to anyone over the age of 13 who's not in 'bad standing with Epic Games'.

By 'bad standing' they mean anyone who's gotten into trouble with the folks that made Fortnite for cheating or bad

THE ROAD TO THE FORTNITE WORLD CUP STARTS HERE.

WEEK 5 FINALS

SOLO

WORLD CUP ONLINE OPEN

OCEANIA

UP NEXT - MORE NA EAST 2:32

TWEET AT US

LINK

QUALIFIED WITH 93 PTS

behaviour, which we're pretty sure you'd never do, because you always play nice in Fortnite. Isn't that right, folks?

While details were sktehcy for many months after the initial announcement Epic Games finally lifted the lid on what fans of the game could expect when the weekly qualifiers launched in April 2019 with ten weekly qualifiers complete with a $1,000,000 prize pool on the line every seven days. These ten qualifiers determined who would make it through to the World Cup Finals in New York City and have a chance at grabbing some of that insane $30,000,000 prize pool fund.

Now, as you know A LOT of people play Fortnite on a daily basis, so to determine who makes it through this is how Epic Games separated the serious players who wanted a shot at the title from the, er, not so serious

players. It all started with Arena Mode, which allowed Players to earn points whenever they want.

Once Players had reached the top of Arena Mode they were automatically entered into the World Cup Online Open Tournaments that took place on weekends. Players then had just three hours to play ten matches in an attempt to grab as many points as possible to reach the top 3,000 in their region and qualify for the Online Open Finals on Sundays.

In the Online Open Finals Epic Games reset Player's scores and once again gave them three hours to play ten matches. Players in the top scoring range grabbed a piece of that $1,000,000 prize pie, while a few lucky ones got invited to the final in New York City in July. Whoa, so no pressure at all? If you think you've got what it takes to be the best, then start practicing for the 2020 Fortnite World Cup today!

WORLD CUP ONLINE OPENS

WORLD CUP FINALS

NEW YORK CITY

SCORE

Fortnite World Cup points system explained.

SOLOS

Victory Royale: 10 Points
2nd-5th: 7 Points
6th-15th: 5 Points
16-25th: 3 Points
Eliminations: 1 Point for each elimination.

DUOS

Victory Royale: 10 Points
2nd-5th: 7 Points
6th-10th: 5 Points
11-15th: 3 Points
Eliminations: 1 Point for each elimination.

NICE SHOT, MAN!

Aiming tips to **help you snag** that coveted Victory Royale in Fortnite Battle Royale!

MOUSE SENSITIVITY

Mouse sensitivity determines how fast your weapon reticule moves. Too fast, you'll wind up spraying bullets everywhere. Too slow, and you'll be taken out of the match by other Players. To find a sweet spot, simply play around with the settings to suit your own playing needs on the battlefield.

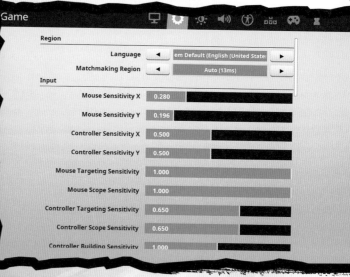

Game

Region

Language	◄ em Default (English (United State ►
Matchmaking Region	◄ Auto (13ms) ►

Input

Mouse Sensitivity X	0.280
Mouse Sensitivity Y	0.196
Controller Sensitivity X	0.500
Controller Sensitivity Y	0.500
Mouse Targeting Sensitivity	1.000
Mouse Scope Sensitivity	1.000
Controller Targeting Sensitivity	0.650
Controller Scope Sensitivity	0.650
Controller Building Sensitivity	1.000

STOP & SHOOT

Don't wildly spray bullets when you come across another Player on the battlefield. You need to be a little mindful when placing a shot because of weapon recoil. Try to find cover before shooting (if you haven't been spotted) otherwise just take a breath and take the shot instead of using up all your ammo.

WEAPON RANGE

Weapon Range is an obvious one – know the limits of the weapon you have in the your hand. For example, you're not going to land long distance headshots with a shotgun. That will require a Sniper Rifle... Or a bazooka to the face! That's why it's good to have multiple weapon types in your arsenal.

PEEK

Peeking is essential for hitting targets in Fortnite Battle Royale. You have to master it if you want to stay alive. It's an easy one to pull off too – simply crouch when near a structure and stand really quickly to see where your target is, before crouching again.

FLICK SHOT

This shot is very important to learn, especially when battling someone at close range. However, it's a tough one to master, so we recommend using Creative Mode to practice it. To pull it off, you have to snap to a target that's off-centre or off-screen from the firing reticule and shoot them.

TARGETING

You see that Player running across the battlefield? Don't aim directly at them if you're going to take the shot. Aim a few feet in front of them to accommodate for the time delay between the bullet leaving your gun and them reaching that spot. Aiming for the shoulders or neck also helps if your target is slow, as you're likely to miss the head.

SPECTACULAR SKINS

Everyone knows character Skins in Fortnite Battle Royale are a big deal. There are so many to choose from, and they come in all different shapes and sizes thanks to the wild imagination of the team at Epic Games, and some cool crossovers with big budget blockbuster movies, such as Avenger and John Wick. Now, these things do cost money so always be sure to check with a grown-up before spending any of your money – or theirs! – on new outfits for characters.

Without further ado, here are some of the best costumes we've seen to date!

1 Blackheart
Hands up anyone who wants to be a pirate? All of you, you say? We thought so! This Legendary Skin was part of the Scallywags set that included the awesome Sea Wolf character outfit, the Buccaneer outfit and the very cool Plunder Glider.

2 Hybrid
Channel your inner ninja warrior with this skin that was released as part of the Brood Set that arrived alongside the Dragon Claw Harvesting Tool, Dragon Stance emote and Hybrid loading screen. The skin came with the Battle Pass for Season 8 and was unlocked at Tier 1.

3 Gemini
Check out this cool Epic Skin. Gemini was released as part of the Space Hops set, which includes the Cryo Hops Back Bling. It comes in two different styles, black and blue, and you can pick it up on the Item Store for 1,500 V-Bucks.

4

Prickly Patroller

Ever wanted to be a cactus? Well, now you can be with the Prickly Patroller Skin. This Uncommon outfit, available for female characters, wasn't released as any part of any set but can be picked up in the Item Store whenever you see it appear.

5

Shaman

This Shaman Skin is actually pretty terrifying, so terrifying we suspect other Players would be scared witless if you came running at them wearing it, while wielding the even scarier Moonbone Harvesting Tool. Grab it for a spooky 1,500 V-Bucks.

6

Nightwitch

Nightwitch is part of the same set that the Shaman was released in. It's called the Moonbone set, and includes the Cuddle Doll and Battle Mask Back Bling. And just like the Shaman this character Skin will set you back 1,500 V-Bucks.

7

Beastmode

This Beastmode Skin is so awesome, and that's because it comes with four different styles. The best part is you get them all by buying just one of the Skins. These variations include, Lion Style, Rhino Style, Jackal Style and Jaguar Style. It costs 1,500 V-Bucks.

8

Psion

Psion is a Rare character Skin that was released as part of the Third Eye set. The pack includes a whole host of funky items, including The Disruptor Back Bling and the Psionic Edge Harvesting Tool. It will set you back a meaty 1,200 V-Bucks if you want to grab it from the Item Store.

9

Kenji

Kenji is an Epic character Skin that's a cross between a mummy and a ninja. It was released as part of The Falcon Clan set, which also includes the Quickstrike Harvesting Tool, and Katana & Kunai Back Bling. If you want it, this one will set you back 1,500 V-Buck.

10

Bandolette

Bandolette is a predator of the Fortnite Battle Royale Island, and you'd better be careful if you see her on the battlefield, because she is ready to kick serious butt. She was released as part of the Rare Tropic Troopers set, and if you want to own the Skin it will cost you 1,200 V-Bucks.

11

Mezmer

Got 1,200 V-Bucks? Then you might want to spend it on this crazy character Skin. Mezmer, an Aztec zombie of sorts, was released as part of the Sun Soldiers set that includes the Sunrise Glider, Axetec Harvesting Tool, and the Sun Wings Back Bling.

12

Cloaked Shadow

Cast a super-ominous shadow over the battlefield with this creepy character Skin that will cost you 1,500 V-Bucks. With black horns, glowing eyes and a weird smoky aura, Cloaked Shadow wasn't part of a set, but does include the awesome Shadow Wings Back Bling.

13

Slushy Soldier

Feeling festive? Then you might want to grab yourself the Slushy Soldier character Skin from the Item Store. This Skin wasn't released as part of a set, but it does include a funky Back Bling called Slushy Jr. If you want it, it'll set you back 1,500 V-Bucks.

14

DJ Bop

Lose yourself in the beat with the DJ Bop Legendary character Skin. This funky female was released as part of the Twin Turntables set alongside the DJ Yonder character Skin, and will set you back 2,000 V-Bucks if you want to add it to your collection of battlefield brawlers.

15

Krampus

Ever heard of Krampus? The half demon, half goat humanoid that runs around dressed as Santa? Well, now you have! This terrifying character from the realm of folklore was released as part of the Krampus set and will cost you a chunk at 2,000 V-Bucks!

16

Reflex

Released as part of the Counterattack set that includes the Pivot Glider, Angular Axe Harvesting Tool and Response Unit Back Bling, Reflex is pretty slick looking. If you'd like to get your hands on it, you'll have to keep an eye on the Item Store and have 1,200 V-Bucks at the ready.

17

Riot

Fortnite Battle Royale goes punk with Riot, a rockin' character Skin that comes complete with Mohawk and a leather jacket covered in metal spikes, so you can't hug this angry dude! He wasn't released as part of a set, and will cost you 1,200 V-Bucks.

18

Tech Ops

Overtake your enemies on the battlefield with the Tech Ops character Skin. Released as part of the Tech Ops set, the Skin was released alongside the Coaxial Copter Glider, Armature Harvesting Tool and The Capacitor Back Bling. Adding it to your collection will set you back 1,200 V-Bucks.

19

The Ice Queen

Long live the scariest Queen of all – The Ice Queen! This sinister looking character Skin was released as part of the Ice Kingdom Set that included the Blue Metallic Wrap, Winter's Thorn Glider, and the Icebringer Harvesting Tool. This one will cost you a pretty hefty 2,000 V-Bucks.

20

Mothmando

Out of the shadows, into the light and ready to bring the fight – say hello to the most brutal bug on the battlefield, Mothmando! He's kind of weird, but we really like this character Skin. Released as part of the Moth Command set, this kooky Skin will cost you a chunky 1,500 V-Bucks.

21

Longshot

Got 1,200 V-Bucks to spend on this character Skin? If so, let's take a look at him. Released as part of the Ranged Recon set, Longshot arrived alongside the Scope Satchel Back Bling, and the Insight female character Skin. Both are super menacing on the battlefield.

22

Shogun

Shogun is a must for anyone out there looking for a super showdown on the battlefield. This armoured warrior features an Oni Mask and a black and gold Kabuto helmet. It's kinda terrifying, and was released as part of the Shogun set. Owning it will cost 2,000 V-Bucks.

23

Spooky Team Leader

This delightfully frightful character Skin features a pretty darn spooky panda-faced getup with green stripes, a pumpkin print on the stomach and a stitched up mouth. Yeah, it's spooky. This one wasn't released as part of a set, and can be picked up on the Item Store for 1,200 V-Bucks.

24

A.I.M.

A.I.M. is so awesome. This robot skin looks a bit like Chappie, and was released as part of the A.I.M. set that included the A.X.E. Harvesting Tool. To nab this you needed to complete the Hunting Party Challenges during Season 6.

25

Summit Striker

Want to be first to the top? Then grab yourself the Fortnite Starter Pack #4 to get your hands on this cool character Skin that's all geared up and ready for climbing the hills on The Island.

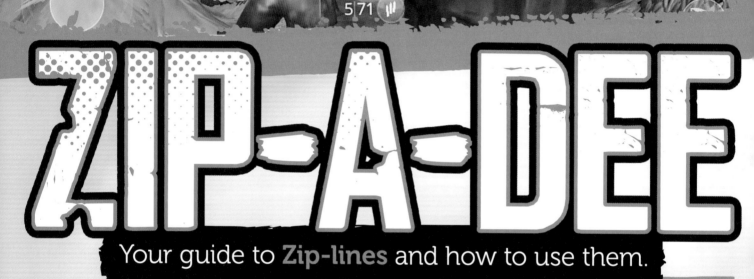

ZIP-A-DEE

Your guide to Zip-lines and how to use them.

There are so many fun and unique ways to speed around the Fortnite Battle Royale Island. There's the Baller, the Driftboard and the All Terrain Karts. And there are these – the Zip-lines, super speedy ways of moving between points on the map. Zip-lines are static forms of transportation that are firmly planted at a number of locations all around the Island map. They never move, and, as much as we would like, they can't be transported around like other items in the game.

Zippy Challenge

When the Zip-lines originally hit the game they featured a number of Challenges alongside them, including having to deal damage to enemy Players on the battlefield while riding a Zip-line. This was a pretty fun, albeit tricky, challenge. If this challenge ever surfaces again; here are some tips to get you through it. Firstly, land in a busy area filled with numerous Zip-Lines. Then be sure to grab a weapon with a high rate of fire. It got insanely hectic the first time around, so we expect it to be the same if the Challenge ever returns from the mysterious Vault.

DOO-DAH

Zipping Rules

Like everything else in the game, Zip-Lines have rules. Zip-lines have two ends that you can move back and forth between as much as you want. There are no limitations as to how many times you can use one. If you're using a Zip-Line and leap off you won't receive any fall damage. That includes leaping from a Zip-Line at maximum height. This means you can pull off some pretty daring attacks on enemies if you leap from a Zip-Line and blast 'em on the way down to Earth. And while Weapons can be used, you can't heal yourself while riding a Zip-Line.

Hints & Tips

Always jump off the Zip-Line before you reach the end of it, because that makes you much less of an easy target. Oh, and don't use your Glider either, because if an enemy is watching from a concealed place you're essentially a sitting duck as you drift back down to the ground. Lastly, before you use a Zip-Line (and while you're riding one) always check your surroundings for enemies. They could be lurking anywhere, watching and waiting for you to drop so they can take you out!

Remember, Fornite fans – Zip-Lines are fun, but you have to respect 'em and use 'em wisely or you might find yourself on the end of an opposing Player's gun!

REBOOT!

Reboot Vans will **change the way you play** Fortnite Battle Royale!

In April of 2019, and clearly in response to emerging Battle Royale hit, Apex Legends, Epic Games introduced a brand new, and very funky, mechanic into the world of Fortnite Battle Royale – the Reboot Van. Delivered with Patch v8.30, the Reboot Van allowed Players to bring back their downed teammates in squad-based modes only. Remember that, folks – it's Duos and Squad Modes only, and not Solo Mode or Limited Time Modes, unless otherwise stated by the developer.

WHERE DID WE PARK THE VAN?

At the time of going to press the Reboot Vans were dotted all around the Fortnite map's main locations, which includes the likes of Snobby Shore, Haunted Hills, Junk Junction, Lucky Landing, Paradise Palms and Salty Springs. Just to be clear, we haven't mentioned all the locations here, so do a little exploring and you'll find plenty more locations on the map where the developer has placed them.

Once you have a solid idea of where the Reboot Vans are located this is how you to revive a downed teammate, and bring them back into the fight for a second chance at grabbing that sweet Victory Royale. When a teammate is taken out of the fight they will drop a Reboot Card. This Reboot Card then needs to be grabbed by either you, or another member of your squad within 90 seconds.

GRAB MY GEAR, PLEASE

Oh, and if you've collected multiple Reboot Cards you can revive multiple Players on the battlefield in one go. Revived Players will then re-enter the match with full health, a Pistol, Light Ammo and Wood. If, however, any surviving Players were smart enough to grab their comrades dropped gear, they can drop it from their inventory to help a friend out!

SUPER FAST CARD COLLECTION

Yes, that's 90 seconds, folks. You need to be fast here, especially if your teammate was foolish and wandered off from the squad only to get themselves blasted by an opponent. And if this is the case be sure to tread carefully, because you could be walking into a trap and wind up getting taken out by your teammate's attacker. Once you have the Reboot Card to hand, you or anyone else on your squad makes a dash for the Reboot Van to revive your squad member.

It's important to note that once you collect the Reboot Card, anyone from the team can use the Reboot Van; it doesn't have to be the person who picked it up. It takes ten seconds for the reboot to kick in, and once a Reboot Van has been used it can't be used again for two full minutes. ●

WONDERFUL WEAPONRY

Check out some of the **best weapons** to wield in Fortnite Battle Royale!

Tactical Shotgun

If you want to get up real close and personal with Players on the battlefield then the Tactical Shotgun is the weapon for you. With just a single shot you can slice off a huge chunk of a rival's health, and swiftly put them down with a second.

Drum Gun

The Drum Gun was one of the most wildly overpowered weapons in the game for a long time. For its sins it was thrown in The Vault, after Players complained about the fact it could shred structures and body armour in seconds. It's currently returned to the game, but with toned down (stopping) power.

Assault Rifle

The Assault Rifle is great for mid-ranged combat. If you can get your hands on an Epic or Legendary tiered one, then you have some serious firepower behind you. These rarities can be pretty hard to find, and usually come in juicy Loot Crates.

Scoped Assault Rifle

Scoped Assault Rifles come in two flavours – Rare and Epic. In Season Eight they were given a little bit of a kick to help them compete against some of the other stronger weapons out there on the battlefield, and since then they've become one of the favourites for Fortnite Battle Royale fans.

Heavy Assault Rifle

The Heavy Assault Rifle is a monster of a gun in Fortnite Battle Royale. It can turn buildings, enemies and vehicles into mulch in a matter of seconds, but you need to play it careful when using it, utilising short, precise bursts of fire. Oh, and the slow reload times leave you open to taking damage.

Supressed SMG

The Suppressed SMG was sent to The Vault back in Season 6, but brought back during Season 7. As it stands this is the only SMG weapon in the game after the Compact SMG got kicked to The Vault in Season 9. It's a solid weapon with considerable stopping power at most ranges.

Mini-Gun

A lot of Players love the Mini-Gun in Fortnite Battle Royale, because it's great for tearing down big structures opponents build. If you get too carried away with spraying bullets everywhere at a pack of enemies, all one of them has to do is find cover and take you out with a headshot.

Supressed Sniper Rifle

The Supressed Sniper Rifle is a thing of beauty, terror in the world of Fortnite Battle Royale. While not quite as powerful as the monstrous Heavy Sniper Rifle, it is still a single round takedown weapon if you can nail that perfect shot. And the fact that it's got a silencer makes it all the more scary.

Hand Cannon

The Hand Cannon is one helluva pistol. It's got insane stopping power, even though this was paired back when the developers tweaked the weapon for a patch released during Season Seven.

Combat Shotgun

The Combat Shotgun can be quite useful in battle given that the reload time is faster than the Tactical shotgun, and it takes two shells at a time. A sort of mash-up of the Tactical and the now Vaulted Heavy Shotgun, this one is perfect for close encounters of the uncomfortable kind.

Rocket Launcher

If there's one weapon on the Fortnite Battle Royale roster that spreads joy it's the Rocket Launcher, especially when Players come across other Fortnite-ers in the midst of a brawl in a large structure. Pulling that trigger, watching it collapse and earning that Victory Royale from a distance is a sweet-tasting Victor Royale.

Grenade Launcher

The Grenade Launcher's greatest gift is its ability to arc rounds at enemies, so one of the best ways to use it is to launch a cluster of 'em at groups of enemies not aware of your presence. If they're well placed, then you've got yourself a wealth of wins right there.

Dynamite

Dynamite was introduced all the way back in November 2018, and then it broke the game for being crazy powerful and found itself thrown into the Vault. It was also part of the excellent Wild West Limited Time Mode, so here's hoping that it makes a return to the game soon.

Boogie Bomb

You'll find Boogie Bombs in Loot Chests and Supply Llamas, or if you're lucky enough to down an opponent holding one in their arsenal. They're funky, they're funny and they'll force your enemies on the battlefield to get down for five full seconds, leaving them open to a blast of bullets.

Burst Assault Rifle

The Burst Assault Rifle is ideal for anyone that struggles with the wild recoil of the other weapons on the list. The very useful Burst capabilities mean that you can fire off a few shots at an enemy, then quickly re-centre your aim before blasting your opponent mere seconds later.

Impulse Grenade

These bad boys can be found in Creative Mode after being sent to the Vault on two different occasions for being too damn powerful. They are found in batches of three and, when thrown, it launches opponents into the air... and sometimes off the edge of a cliff if you time it correctly!

ROLLIN' ROLLIN' ROLLIN'

Have yourself a ba[ll] in Fortnite Battle Royale' Baller!

here's no doubt in our mind that the team at Epic Games were sitting watching Jurassic World one weekend, and then came to work on [...] with the idea of integrating The Baller into the [...] Fortnite Battle Royale. It's practically the same vehicle park visitors used to ride around the island... before the dinosaurs went nuts (again) and started eating tourists (again). It's a cool vehicle, and with th[e] addition of a built-in Grappler, you can use The Balle[r] to get around easily.

BALLER SPOTS

The developers have been quite generous dropping The Baller throughout the map. You'll find them parked up at Frosty Flights, Polar Peak, next to Shifty Shafts, Pleasant Park, Lonely Lodge and at pretty much all of the larger outposts on the Island. Once you find one, here's a few things to remember – they're a single seat, you won't take any damage for falling, and you're pretty much impervious to damage once you're inside it with the exception of being caught inside a Storm.

SQUISHY STUFF

You can even use The Grappler to grab an enemy and roll over them. If they're wearing a lot of armour it might take a couple of attempts to knock them out of the match, but it's still pretty funny rolling right over 'em during a big brawl. The Baller, if moving fast enough, can also smash into structures. Again, it might take a few attempts to break down a particularly tough structure, so be sure to always move around if you're trying to take down something with other Players inside. ●

ROLL AWAY

It's a pretty awesome vehicle thanks to that 360 Degree protection, and with a huge Health Bar you can survive for quite some time in it if you play it smart and, er, roll away from trouble whenever you find yourself being chased by a Player. Just like when you're using the Driftboard be sure to swerve from side to side as much as possible when you're being shot at. It will likely save your life! With the Grappler connected to it you can use it to climb high structures and survey the map without the fear of being blasted from behind by a sneaky opposing Player.

DRIFT KING

Check out the Fortnite Battle Royale Driftboard!

Released alongside the Drifting Limited Time Mode, the Driftboard is a sort of futuristic snowboard that looks a lot like the hoverboards that appeared in the fantastic film, Back To The Future II all the way back in 1989. If you haven't seen it we highly recommend checking out that masterpiece of cinema. It's available on Netflix!

The Driftboard Limited Time Mode that was released in Season Seven was a great way to introduce the board by pitting Players against each other on the boards as they fought it out in squads. It was fast and furious, plus you really had to master the skill of aiming with everyone moving so speedily on the battlefield.

Board Battles

One of the best things about the Driftboard is that it's pretty silent. That means you can sneak up on unsuspecting enemies at speed if they haven't spotted you. You can also revive teammates without having to jump off, but you can't build anything while cruising around, which does make sense... Er, in a game where you fly hoverboards, and parachute onto an island from a flying bus.

If you find yourself facing down an enemy one of the best ways to tackle them is to dash forward using Boost Mode, then leap into the air and shoot them. If you're taking fire from an opponent the best way to avoid that gunfire is by zigzagging left and right on the board before quickly taking a few shots of your own.

The Driftboards are fun, and while they do take a little mastering they can be an awesome addition to your arsenal and that eternal quest for Victory Royales! ●

Where To Find 'Em

Driftboards are dotted all over the map, in particular on the snowy areas of the Island including Shifty Shafts, Polar Peak, Happy Hamlet and Frosty Heights. Other locations where you'll find small clusters include Tilted Towers, and near the woods close to Sunny Steps. There are plenty to go around for all, and definitely something you should consider mastering, because they are a lot of fun.

You can pull off a number of ice cool moves on the Driftboard. Firstly, it's got a Boost Mode that allows you to whip across surfaces at lightning speeds while chasing after (or running from) other Players. You can also perform some pretty slick jumps while using it, and given that your hands are free it's the only vehicle in the game at the time of going to press that allows you to shoot or throw items.

ISLAND LIFE

The **complete guide to listed locations** in Fortnite Battle Royale!

Haunted Hills

Haunted Hills is a good spot for a solo landing. It's filled with plenty of items to harvest, and there are multiple chests dotted around the place, including deep inside the mausoleum. However, if you do drop here as a squad you need to be careful, because there are generally not enough things for everyone to grab.

Junk Junction

Junk Junction is crammed with metal to harvest! If you drop here don't forget to take the time to climb on top of the piles of cars and wrecks to check for goodies. If you want to explore the area head to the Southeast towards the middle of the map and you might find a Loot Chest crammed with lots of Legendary Items.

Loot Lake

If you are after loads of loot then hit up Loot Lake. This area houses a massive vault where all the weapons are sent to when they're not being used in the game, as well as a number of other buildings dotted all around it. Be sure to check the area for Loot Chests, but be sure to keep an eye out for hordes of Players dropping here.

Lucky Landing

Lucky Landing is decked out in a cool Asian theme, and oddly, not a whole lot of people tend to drop there. That means you should consider landing there, because the Loot can be plentiful. However, and given that we've just told you, and everybody else too, we suspect it might become quite popular!

Fatal Fields

Fatal Fields is a large farm filled with old barns, stables, a pond and a scattering of crop fields. At the start of Season 6 the corn had grown to its full height, which makes it a great place to hide, collect Loot and generally wait it out for a while. There's a small quarry in the area too, which is good for grabbing building stuff.

Mega Mall

This area of the map houses a huge futuristic retail complex and a car park, as well as residential buildings. It used to be called Retail Row, but that changed when the developers built the Mall at the start of Season 9. The Mega Mall feature comes with cool tie-ins to Stranger Things: Season 3, including portals to the Upsidedown world!

Sunny Steps

Located at the foot of the Volcano, Sunny Steps was once called Wailing Woods. It replaced the original location during Season 8 of Fortnite Battle Royale. It's now an Aztec city of sorts that's filled with plenty of Loot that can be grabbed by checking out the pyramids and campfire sites scattered about the area.

Salty Springs

Salty Springs is a pretty sizeable town nestled right there in the middle of the map. There are always plenty of materials to harvest here, and the houses tend to have great Loot, especially in the attic area. There's a bunker tucked away in the Blue House, and there tends to be a handful of Quadcrashers kicking around too.

The Block

The Block is, well, it's a Block. This thing replaced Risky Reels back in Season 7. It's pretty cool, because each week the best creations from the fun Creative Mode are featured here for you to go and explore. Other than that, there's not much to grab here during a Solo match save for the odd Loot Chest or two.

Shifty Shafts

Shifty Shafts is an old underground mineshaft loaded with drifts, cages and trucks, as well as incredibly tight areas that you'll have to manoeuvre around with extreme caution. With that in mind be sure to try and grab a Tactical Shotgun for close encounters, because you'll last a lot longer, especially in the spooky tunnels.

Paradise Palms

Replacing Moisty Mire at the outset of Season Five, Paradise Palms' coolest feature is that it houses a racetrack where you can challenge friends or other players to a race using either Shopping Carts or the All Terrain Kart. But in Season 6 all ATKs were removed from the surrounding area, so remember that!

Lazy Lagoon

Formerly Lazy Links AND Anarchy Acres, Lazy Lagoon is a small lagoon with a big ol' pirate ship parked right there in the middle of it. There are some small surrounding islands with buildings and a little bit of Loot. The area is covered with Canons, because, well, it's got a pirate ship in it.

Dusty Divot

Formerly known as Dusty Depot, Dusty Divot was completely transformed when a meteor crash-landed in the area during Season Four of Battle Royale. Gone is the industrial area that was once loaded with loot, and in its place is a research station overrun with plant life. Dusty Divot is still a great looting spot!

Happy Hamlet

Happy Hamlet was once the Flush Factory, the home of beautiful toilet bowls and industrial buildings. Now it's a small European town that was added in Season 7 along with a whole heap of snow. It used to be a very popular area to land, but not so much now. Still, you'll find Zip Lines and a good selection of Loot here.

Lonely Lodge

This place is an ideal place to drop into if you want to scout the surrounding areas. It's got a huge watchtower, and if you land fast enough you might be able to grab the Loot Chests dotted around the area. There are also Blue Mushrooms scattered about, so grab those to power up your shield before entering the fight.

Snobby Shores

Snobby Shores is a sketchy place to drop, because it's almost never located inside the eye of the Storm. That means when it hits, you're going to have to do some running to reach the safe area. Still, if you drop here there's plenty to take a look at, including the, err, massive Viking ship sat atop the mountain.

Pleasant Park

Located to the northwest of the map, Pleasant Park is a quite a popular drop spot for Players; so check your surroundings when landing here. There are lots of looting opportunities in the houses spread out around the area, as well as in the gas station, and the route towards Neo Tilted.

Neo Tilted

Neo Tilted was previously known as Tilted Towers. It's absolutely brimming with loot, but loot that comes at a very steep price... in the form of other players! Almost everyone drops here at the start of a match, which means you'll find yourself in lots of close combat situations. Pro tip: pack a Tactical Shotgun when you stay at Neo Tilted.

Pressure Plant

The Pressure Plant sits atop the Volcano that exploded in Season 8. If you do decide to land there you'll find a whole stack of Metal to harvest for building things during the match, as well as quite a number of Loot Chests containing plenty of gear. Stay frosty though, people tend to gravitate towards the area because its quiet.

Polar Peak

Polar Peak is the iceberg that smashed into the island all the way back at the start of Season 7's festive celebrations in 2018. Over time the landscape has changed, and at the time of going to press there was a huge crack appearing in the area after the Volcano erupted. It could be gone before we finish writing this!

TOYS, TOYS, TOYS!

Fortnite toys are awesome. There are just so many to choose from, so to help you choose which one is perfect for that birthday or Christmas list here's a whole heap of figures, play sets and NERF guns to ogle over and decide upon. Enjoy!

Fortnite Squad Mode 4 Figure Pack

Hands up who wants a killer four pack of figures featuring four of the most popular character skins ever in Fortnite Battle Royale? Everyone? We thought so! This pack of Epic and Legendary character skins includes Rex, Cuddle Team Leader, Ragnarok and Brite Bomber. And they all have guns. Lots of 'em!

Fortnite Battle Royale Collection Battle Bus

Have you ever wanted to cruise around in your very own version of the Battle Bus? Well, now you can! This slick set comes with two exclusive figures called Burnout and Victory Umbrella. These two brawlers can ride inside the bus along with the huge collection of additional figures that are for sale separately.

Fortnite Turbo Builder Set

The Fortnite Turbo Builder Set is something else, that's for sure. It comes complete with Raven and Jonesy action figures, 27 wood building materials, 27 stone building materials, 27 metal building materials, 4 weapons, and 2 harvesting tools. Having all this cool stuff means you and your friends can build your own Fortnite forts!

Fortnite Single Panel Duvet Cover

Playing Fortnite can be pretty exhausting stuff, so imagine how cool it would be to turn off that console or gaming device and hit the hay – in a bed clad in Fortnite bed sheets! This fantastic set comes complete with pillow case cover, and a duvet cover. Oh, and it's reversible too!

Fortnite Battle Royale Mega Fort Set

Fortnite Battle Royale Mega Fort Set is perfect for storing Fortnite mini figures. Plus, the wood, brick, and metal panels can be used to construct three different forts. The set also comes complete with Tricera Ops and Blue Squire action figures, which means you can stage your very own Fortnite battle in your room!

Fortnite Loot Collectible Chest

Opening Loot Chests in Fortnite Battle Royale is super-exciting, right? Well, now you can experience the excitement of cracking one open in real life with the Fortnite Loot Collectible Chest. There are six to collect in total, and each one includes weapons, back bling and wood building materials. Pretty damn cool!

NERF Fortnite Llama Microshots Blaster

Want to blast someone with a teeny weeny dart? Then get yourself the NERF Fortnite Llama Microshots Blaster! Inspired by the wacky loot box, this nifty NERF gun fires one dart at a time, doesn't require any batteries and is part of a slick series of Fortnite: Battle Royale Microshot Blasters.

SOMETHIN STRANGE

That time Fortnite Battle Royale met
Netflix's Stranger Things

kay, so unless you've been living under a rock for the last twelve months you'll have probably heard of little show on an up and coming streaming service called, Netflix. That show is Stranger Things. Arguably the most enjoyable thing lovers of eighties pop culture have seen since, well, the end of the eighties, Stranger Things Season 3 smashed viewing records and blew everyone away.

It's really no surprise then that given Fortnite Battle Royale's super cool crossovers with the likes of The Avengers and John Wick, that Netflix and Epic Games teamed up to introduce a whole host of goodies from the show to the world of Fortnite.

Portals

It all started back in July of 2019 just before the premiere of Season 3 of the show when strange portals started appearing all over the Mega Mall. Netflix and Epic Games had hinted at the collaboration beforehand, and when Players discovered that one of the eateries in the food court of the Mall was called Scoops Ahoy - the very same name of the ice cream parlour from the show – everyone began to suspect something was up, and a crossover was imminent.

Then, all of a sudden weird portals started popping up all over the map. The very same portals that appear in the TV series that allow characters to travel between the real world and the Upside Down! When Players took a step inside these creepy things they were teleported around the Mall much to their amusement.

Stranger Skins

On July 4 the Stranger Things and Fortnite Battle Royale crossover kicked into overdrive when Twitter went wild with announcements revealing some very cool character Skins for Players to get their hands on, including Skins modelled on Chief Hopper and the absolutely terrifying Demogorgon! Imagine running around the battlefield as the Demogorgon? You wouldn't need a weapon, because people would just run off in terror!

There was also some slick Weapon Wraps in the shape of the spooky vines from the TV series that you could also get your hands on. The character Skins, at the time of going to press, cost between 1, 2000 and 1,500 V-Bucks. Once the promotion ended they were removed from the Item Store and placed in The Vault, so we hope that you managed to snag them for yourself if you were a fan. If not, we suspect they might be back for Season 4 of Stranger Things! ●

RETAIL ROW

Check out the official Fortnite Battle Royale online store!

Fortnite isn't just a game. It's a crazy popular global brand, and given how successful it's been since it launched back in 2017, it's no surprise that a slew of cool merchandise and team ups with popular brands have appeared over the last two super busy years for the team at Epic Games.

The company has now taken its awesome merchandise business to the next level by launching its own official store that's been aptly titled, Retail Row, after the popular location in the game. The store itself opened just in time for Christmas 2018, and we're pretty certain that it was a very busy time for the Fortnite merchandise team that year!

There's so much cool stuff to choose from including T-Shirts, hoodies and onesies ranging in price from £20.00 to £55.00, so you might want to a) start saving all your pocket money, b) ask your parents for a loan or c) put it on your Christmas list!

Let's take a look at some of the cool stuff for sale on Retail Row right now.

DURR BURGER ONESIE

If you're after a super cozy onesie based on the infamous fast food restaurant in the world of Fortnite Battle Royale, than this Durr Burger getup is most definitely for you! It comes in a variety of sizes and will set you back a meaty £55.00. Pricey!

DRIFT TEE
£20.00

FORTNITE PURPLE/BLACK LOGO TEE
£20.00

FORTNITE STITCHED LOGO TEE
£20.00

FORTNITE BLACK/BLUE LOGO TEE
£20.00

FORTNITE BLACK/PINK LOGO TEE
£20.00

FORTNITE BLACK/LAVENDER LOGO TEE
£20.00

TEAM PIZZA SWEATSHIRT

Now you too can fly the Tomato Head outfit flag in the real world with this wild and wacky looking sweatshirt. It's also a cool nod to the awesome Food Fight Limited Time Mode. If you want this one be prepared to dish out a cool £39.99.

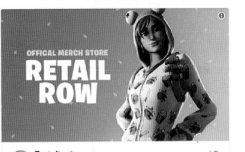

GREEN BUSH TEE

The Green Bush is one of the funniest Fortnite items you can get your hands on in the game, and yet we're also betting the Legendary Rarity item has saved lots of lives on the battlefield! So what better way to salute it than with a T-shirt?

SKULL TROOPER TEE – BLACK

The Skull Trooper is arguably one of the most terrifying character skins in the entire game. And that's probably why it's also so damn popular! Now you can sport the Skull Trooper scary face on this cool T-shirt for £20.00.

SKULL TROOPER PULLOVER

Okay, so this is the second item on the list that features the Skull Trooper – but just look at it, and its awesome super-scariness! This pocket hoodie just screams 'Don't mess with me' to anyone who plays Fortnite Battle Royale. Grr!

DURRR BURGER YELLOW OVERSIZED TEE
£20.00

GREEN BUSH TEE
£20.00

DJ YONDER PURPLE TEE
£20.00

HANG TIME

Take a look at some of the most stylish **Gliders** in Fortnite Battle Royale!

1 Avengers Quinjet

The Quinjet is one of the coolest jets in all of comic book movie history. To nab it you had to be quick, because it was only ever released as part of the Endgame Limited Time Mode that celebrated Avengers Endgame's cinematic release back in April 2019.

2 The Milano

This awesome Glider skin really needs no introduction, but just in case you're one of the few that doesn't recognise it it's The Milano from Guardians of the Galaxy. Duh! This was released in time to celebrate Endgame's world conquering cinematic run, and it is a must-own!

3 Choppa

Want to look tough flying onto the battlefield? Then get to the Store and buy a Choppa! Clearly a nod in name to the classic sci-fi terror tale, Predator. The Choppa Glider was released as part of the Tropic Troopers set, which in itself is likely a nod to the movie, Tropic Thunder.

4 Flappy Flyer

Released as part of the Fowl Play Set (get it?) this wacky yellow chicken is probably the strangest Glider in our list. You control this thing with the fork and spoon attached to the chicken's feet, and, well, that's about it. Wacky indeed!

5 Laser Chomp

How cool is this Glider, folks? Who wouldn't want to fly into battle on The Island on a shark...with a laser attached to its head? It's so crazy cool, right? Released as part of the Chomp Set this one will cost you 1,500 V-Bucks and it's so worth it!

6 Umbrella

It may look plain and simple, but believe us when we say the Umbrella Glider is one of the most important Gliders you'll unlock in the world of Fortnite Battle Royale? Why? Because you only get it once you've snagged a Victory Royale!

7 Venus Flyer

Chomp, chomp, chomp! Say hello to the Venus Flyer. This sharp-toothed Glider skin hit Fortnite Battle Royale back in the summer of 2018 alongside the super creepy character skin, Flytrap, and can be bought for 1,200 V-Bucks.

8 Jolly Roger

Arr, yer filthy landlubbers! This here be the Jolly Roger, a highly sought after Glider that first debuted at Christmas 2017 on the Fortnite Store. It'll cost filthy scallywags such as yerselves a meagre 500 V-Bucks. Yarr!

9 Servo

This Epic Rarity Glider will cost you 1,200 V-Bucks. It comes complete with a super cool design that combines a stylish propeller system with aerodynamic design. It's very future-chic and came as part of the Archetype skin set that was released in August 2018.

10 Orbital Shuttle

Released as part of the Space Explorers Set alongside the Deep Space Lander, the Orbital Shuttle is a pretty sweet Glider that goes really well with the Leviathan character skin. If you want to get your hands on this one it'll cost 1,200 V-Bucks.

SAVIN' THE WORLD

Okay, so the entire world is pretty much playing Fortnite Battle Royale these days. One of the reasons for this is that it's free. It doesn't cost anything to download, whereas the original base game - which existed before the Battle Royale Mode was added - does cost money. Released back in the summer of 2017, Fortnite Save The World comes in a variety of flavours and prices.

At the time of going to press it will cost you £32.99 for The Standard Founders Pack, or £49.99 for the Deluxe Founders Pack. Epic Games had promised that the entire game was supposed to transition to a Free-To-Play business model in 2018, but that has since been pushed back to an undisclosed date for reasons unknown.

How does it work?

Fortnite Save The World features a pretty cool story for you to sink your teeth into. A huge chunk of the world's population has vanished after a giant purple storm appeared out of

GIFT BOX!

nowhere, and brought about the End of Days. And with that storm came the monsters, or Husks. The survivors of this bizarre apocalyptic event have discovered how to build things called Storm Shields, which clear the strange purple clouds and reduce the number of Husk attacks on the planet.

This is where you come in – you play the role of Base Leader, and your job is to rescue survivors, expand the Storm Shield, and kick some serious Husk butt while trying to, well, Save The World, of course. All the great things you love about the Fortnite Battle Royale mode are present here, including building and wicked weaponry, but with the added twist of monsters, lots of zany monsters!

Skill trees & V-Bucks

There is a lot to take in when you first jump into Save The World. The Skill Trees can seem quite daunting at first, but take your time to get to know your way around upgrading and enhancing your roster of playable

characters so that you can pick the right character for the many different missions you'll embark on.

One of the major plusses of owning a copy of Save The World is that it's pretty much one of the best ways to farm V-Bucks without having to consistently spend real-world money. It's not easy though, and you'll have to be prepared to put the hours in taking on all of the Daily Quests, missions, side quests and challenges.

Decisions, decisions

Fortnite Save The World isn't cheap, and it is not necessary to own a copy to get the most out of your

experience with Fortnite Battle Royale. While Epic Games hasn't mentioned anything about a potential date for moving the game to the world of Free-To-Play at the time of going to press, it might be worth hanging on a little longer before spending your hard earned money on the full priced game. Or just go ahead and do what we did and pop it on a Christmas list! ●

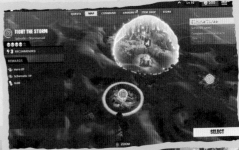

71

WRAP PARTY

Check out these super styl-ee Wraps for your weapons and vehicles!

1 VALENTINE

Spread the love on the battlefield with the Fortnite Valentine Wrap. This one was released during the Valentine's Day 2019 and Players earned it by completing the Overtime Challenges set out in Season 7, which means you can't buy this one from the Store.

2 RIVET

The Rivet Wrap hit the Fortnite Item Store back in March 2019 as part of the Waypoint Set, which included the superb Signal Hub Back Bling and scary looking Waypoint character Skin. To buy it on its own will cost you 300 V-Bucks.

3 SPRINKLES

Add a little flavour to your weaponry and Harvesting Tool with the Sprinkles Wrap! Released as part of the Two Scoops set that included a whole heap of tasty treats, such as the Ice Cream Cruiser Glider and Sno Cone Back Bling.

4 SUNPRINT

Released as part of the wild looking Sun Soldiers set that included the Sunbird and Mezmer character Skins that arrived with the Season 8 Battle Pass. The Sunprint could be unlocked by working your way through the Battle Pass Challenges and reaching Tier 43.

5 ULTRA RED

You want some red Wrapping for your vehicles and weaponry? Sure you do. In fact, what you want is Ultra Red! It's not just red...it's Ultra, and that is why it's on our list of essential Wraps. Released as part of the Season 7 Battle Pass the Ultra Wrap is ultra awesome!

7 LUCKY

Celebrate the most Irish of holidays by turning all of your weapons and vehicles into lucky charms with the Lucky Wrap. Released just in time for St. Patrick's Day 2019, this one is of Uncommon Rarity and will set you back a modest 300 V-Bucks.

6 DRAGON SCALES

Terrify your enemies on the battlefield with Dragon Scales! This one was released at the very end of February 2019 as part of the Brood Set that also included the Hybrid character Skin, Dragon's Claw Harvesting Tool and a Dragon Stance emote.

8 CANDY CANE

Candy Cane was the very first Wrap to be made available to fans in the Item Store during Christmas 2018. It costs 300 V-Bucks and adds a pretty damn cheery festival vibe to any Player's vehicles, weapons or Harvesting Tool.

10 DISCO

Disco, disco, disco! Released on the 13th day of the 14 Days of Fortnite Challenge, the Disco Wrap is a Rare cosmetic item that adds a little bling to your weapons and Harvesting Tool on the battlefield. Consider it funky stuff, folks!

9 CUDDLE HEARTS

Cuddle Hearts Wrap hit Fortnite Battle Royale in celebration of Valentine's Day and the Share The Love event back in February 2018. To get their hands on this one all Players had to do was enter a Creator Code into Fortnite, and hey presto – owned!

CLASSIC COMBAT

Let's take a look at Fortnite Battle Royale's **Unvaulted Limited Time Mode!**

There are so many Limited Time Modes that have been introduced by the developers since the game launched all the way back in 2017. We have covered numerous ones in previous annuals, but Classic might just turn out to be a favourite amongst you. Why? Because it brings back all of the cool weapons that have been sent to The Vault for whatever reason Epic Games deemed fit. Boo! Hiss!

The Limited Time Mode itself is quite simple. There is nothing complicated about this one – you are dropped onto The Island and numerous weapons that you haven't had a chance to wield in eons are back on the battlefield for you to snag, and hunt down rival Players with. It's that simple. There are no complicated mechanics here. Just grab a gun. Find another Player. Point. Aim. And shoot!

HAPPY HOLIDAYS

The Mode itself isn't fresh for 2019. It was released back in 2018 during the 14 Days of Fortnite that crash landed onto consoles, mobile and home computers during the holidays, and as we said previously it doesn't change the basic gameplay tenet of how you've been tackling Fortnite Battle Royale.

You can play the Limited Time Mode solo, or in Squads, depending on your preference. If you want to grab that sweet, sweet Victory Royale on your own, then we understand you're more a of Solo Player, but if you like to team up with pals, then form a Squad!

SMART GUNPLAY

While it's all well and good that you get to play with weapons that have been vaulted from the game for some time, these shooters were removed from the world of Fortnite Battle Royale for a reason. That means you will have to take round or two to get to grips with things such as stopping power, range and rate of fire. You should also make sure you have enough Shields and Health Packs in your Inventory before wading into a brawl with another Squad or Player.

Weapons featured in the Limited Time Mode include the Scoped Assault Rifle to the Pump Shotgun. Scoped Revolver, Remote Explosives, Light Machine Gun, Bottle Rockets and Chiller Grenade. We're still waiting on The Crossbow and the Old SMG to be introduced to the Mode, so here's hoping the team will include them at some point down the line when Unvaulted Limited Time Mode returns.

MAN IN BLACK

John Wick enters the Fortnite Battle Royale contest!

J ohn Wick's Bounty Limited Time Mode may have only lasted a few days in the world of Fortnite Battle Royale, but it was probably one of the best examples of just how tuned in the developers are to what's going on in the world of pop culture. The event didn't just include a new mode to play around in, it also included skins, Back Bling, a Harvesting Tool and two brand new guns that were literally lifted from the world of the kick-ass movie and transplanted into the game.

GUNS, GUNS, GUNS!

These two new weapons are the Tactical Assault Rifle and the Combat Shotgun which John Wick wields like a champ in the action-packed movies. While the Tactical Assault Rifle was awesome to wield, the Combat Shotgun was far too overpowered, and would cut through enemies like they were warm butter. So, how did the mode work? Sit back and let us tell you the story of how John Wick and Fortnite worked hand-in-hand to create one of the best modes in the game.

HUNT HIGH VALUE TARGETS
PLAYERS WITH THE TOP 3 BOUNTIES WILL BE SHOWN ON THE MAP & COMPASS.

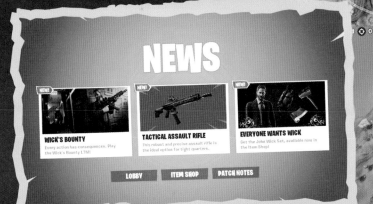

NICE SUIT!

Players are dropped into the island just like every other match in Fortnite Battle Royale, only this time they land with the Combat Shotgun and Tactical Assault Rifle, which means looting isn't actually that important. What it does is up the ante straight away by allowing players to engage in intense action instantly. Players have three lives and three gold coins. If you get whacked you lose your coins. If you whack another player, then you get their coins. The goal in John Wick's Bounty is to amass 500 gold coins in total to win this insanely wild match.

COMING TO GET YA!

However, the first, second and third ranking players in the match are visible to other players on the map, which really lay on the pressure. It also meant that things could take a turn for the worse at the drop of a hat. A low ranking player could take out the top-ranking player if they got lucky, and with players possessing three lives it also meant that matches felt much longer than standard Battle Royale modes. It's a real shame that the mode lasted for only a short time, but here's hoping John Wick will return time and time again to the world of Limited Time Modes! ●

YOUR MISSION IS TO EARN *GOLD TOKENS* BY ELIMINATING ENEMY PLAYERS.

WISH YOU WERE HERE